COLLEEN PETES

AUDIENCE

The Perfect Guide to Building Your Audience, Learn All the Essentials on How to Attract Attention and Build Your Audience, and Create Content that Gets Shared

Descrierea CIP a Bibliotecii Naţionale a României
COLLEEN PETES
 **AUDIENCE. The Perfect Guide to Building Your Audience,
Learn All the Essentials on How to Attract Attention and Build
Your Audience, and Create Content that Gets Shared** / Colleen
Petes. – Bucharest: Editura My Ebook, 2020
 ISBN

COLLEEN PETES

AUDIENCE

The Perfect Guide to Building Your Audience, Learn All the Essentials on How to Attract Attention and Build Your Audience, and Create Content that Gets Shared

My Ebook Publishing House
Bucharest, 2020

TABLE OF CONTENTS

INTRODUCTION

Have you ever dreamed of running a business from home, writing about topics that you love?

Do you already have a business that you want to bring more customers to?

Or maybe you just want to make a difference and have a message you want to share?

Either way, the web is the best place to do this and thanks to the internet we now have the means to contact anyone on the planet and to reach a huge audience with whatever message we want to share.

Unfortunately though, so does everyone else.

And this is where the problem comes in: standing out is *incredibly* difficult with there being such a wealth of content and information available on the web. So how do you go about getting noticed and standing out when we live in such a *noisy* world?

That's the challenge of any modern blogger and it's what we're going to be looking at in this ebook. By the end, you'll know exactly how to break through the chatter as though you had your very own foghorn!

What You Will Learn

Standing out online is more important today than ever before. The days of direct ads are now firmly behind us and studies show that a Tweet or social media post from the right person is now much more valuable than even a prime time advert on television.

But people are getting savvy and if you're going to get noticed you need to start seeing differently. In a world that's full of constant overstimulation, many of us now suffer from 'banner blindness'. Trying to get someone to sit up and take notice of you is the name of the game and you won't do that by using the same tired methods that worked 10, 5 or even 2 years ago.

In this book you'll learn precisely how to differentiate yourself from all the other voices on the web and how to get the *right* people to sit up and take notice of your message. You'll find out:

- How to find the 'route to market'

- How to select the right niche and the right 'sized pond'

- How to create high quality content that people *want* to read

- Why some content thrives more than the rest

- The power of narrative

- How to create your own platform

- How to build up a huge social media following

- Why some content gets shared

- How to grow your audience Are you ready to start *being heard?*

The Landscape: Stats & Facts

Before we dive straight in, let's first take a look at 'the lay of the land'. The statistics surrounding internet marketing right now can tell us a great deal about what's working and what isn't and about how best to approach your online marketing.

Here are some statistics for 2016:

- 91% of internet users own a PC or laptop

- 80% of internet users own a smartphone

- 47% own a tablet

- 37% use a games console

- That said – more traffic now comes from mobile than any other platform

- Facebook now has more active users than the population of China

- YouTube is the second largest 'search engine'

- But in terms of traditional search engines, Bing is right behind Google with 21% of the market share

- That goes up to around 30% if you include Yahoo! (which is powered by Bing)

- Instagram is the second largest social media platform behind Facebook

- Email marketing is the form of marketing with the highest ROI

- 84% of American adults use the internet

This gives us a little bit of a 'snapshot' of the way the web is being used today and in turn will help us when we come onto the next chapters and start looking at how we're going to find, reach and be heard by our particular segment of that audience.

CHAPTER 1

BE WHERE YOUR AUDIENCE IS HANGING OUT

Our first step is to 'be where our audience is'. But on top of this, we're also going to have to first identify and possibly even choose our audience.

If you already have a business or a website, then your audience will already be selected. You've likely already put a lot of work into your online presence and you probably won't want to start again from scratch. That means you already have your audience and you just need to find where they are.

But if you *don't* already have your business model, then that means that you can take a step back at this point and choose what audience you're going to target. Because as we'll learn, some audiences are certainly easier to find that others.

Your audience you see, is going to be entirely dependent on the topic of your website or blog; or the nature of your product or service.

If you're selling surf boards, then your audience is likely to be young people in their teens and 20s, who probably live near a beach somewhere.

Conversely, if you're selling a weight loss plan for vegetarians, then your audience is: vegetarians.

Your product/topic informs your audience and your audience defines your product or service.

If you haven't yet chosen your audience, then that means that you can design your product and your website with this point in mind.

What Makes a Great Audience?

So if you *do* have the luxury of choosing your audience, what kind of audience should you pick?

The ideal here is always going to be an audience that is large enough for you to make a lot of potential sales/money from advertising, while still being small enough that you can reach them directly. You also want to pick an audience that isn't already overly saturated with marketing.

So to quite simply answer the main question poised in this text: How do you stand out in a noisy world?

One answer is: *go where it's less noisy.*

In other words, if your plan is to create a generic fitness website, then you should be aware that you just made yourself a massive uphill struggle. The simple act of picking a topic that is so widely appreciated now means that you don't have a very 'specific' audience to target. You now have to target pretty much *everyone* which makes your focus far broader and far less specific.

At the same time, by having a niche that is so popular, you are now going head-to-head with millions of other websites. You'll be taking on Bodybuilding.com directly for instance and any number of famous fitness and health bloggers. This is a huge undertaking as you're now going up against a massive number of competitors and trying to stand out in an area where there are many other companies spending thousands or even millions of dollars on their advertising.

On the other hand though, if you were able to find a much smaller market that wasn't being catered to, then you could reach them directly, offer them something they can't get anywhere else and then quickly corner that market.

The only problem with this strategy is that you'll now very quickly run out of potential customers and no longer be able to grow.

The trick is to find an audience that's big enough to help you meet your goals but not so saturated that it's impossible to stand out.

One great strategy is to aim a small cross section of a much larger audience. So for example, this might mean that you create a blog on 'fitness for vegetarians', or 'fitness for kids'. In doing this, you have now taken a huge audience that you can grow into, but you've given yourself a small, focussed demographic *within* that much bigger area. You can later branch out and start bringing in more potential customers in future.

Of course you also need to think about the *kind* of audience you're going to be targeting and the kind of audience that will once again help you to meet your goals. It's not just about the *size* of that demographic and the accessibility; it's also about whether these are the kinds of people who are loyal fans, the kinds of people who buy products online and the kinds of people with disposable income. Of course the perfect reader for your blog is someone who will sign in every day and who will be tempted to buy the products that you put in front of them!

Spend some time surveying your audience therefore and doing market research. Assess the competition, look at their buying habits and then ask yourself if you would do better to slightly broaden or narrow your scope.

Finding Your Route to Market

Once you have your audience, you have your market.

The next thing to do is to think about the title of this chapter: 'being where your audience is hanging out'.

What that means, is that you have to *find* your audience. And the best way to do this is to find a 'route to market'.

Route to market is a business term that basically means a direct access point to the kind of person who is right for your website/business. If you can *find* a route to market, then you can almost guarantee profit.

Because really, the simple truth of any content marketing strategy or even any business model is that you're trying to identify an audience, create something you can sell to them and then *put that thing in front of that audience*. When you simplify it like this, it really is a very easy process – you just need a way to connect group X with product/website Y.

Note that television is not a route to market – that's just a platform through which you market.

A route to market is something that much more specifically leads to that exact audience.

So a perfect example would be an industry magazine. If you have a website about gardening and you're selling gardening tools, then a gardening magazine would be an *ideal* route to market. So too would be gardening forum.

And the easiest way to start a business and to start making money is to select a small, uncatered-for audience that you *already* have access to. So think about your existing contacts and resources: do you know the editors of any magazines? Do you know any top bloggers or YouTube vloggers?

Do you happen to be head of a fan club? Do you lecture at a University on a given subject?

Now you just need to create the product and blog for *that* audience and you have a fool proof recipe! Don't make life difficult for yourself: take the path of least resistance, use existing contacts and target the most responsive groups.

And if the area that you have access too isn't in the niche that you want to work with, see this as a starting point and use it to begin your growth. Once you've conquered one small niche/industry, you can move on to the next.

Know Your Audience

But what if you genuinely don't already have any contacts you can turn into routes to market?

Or what if you have exhausted those options/don't want to go that route?

The next step is to profile your audience. In marketing, we refer to something called a 'persona'. A persona is an imaginary biography that describes the ideal kind of person you're writing for and the ideal kind of person that you want to sell to/attract to your website.

So if we're going back to the gardening magazine, then your persona might be an older man, nearing retirement age. Or then again, if you took my earlier advice and decided to aim for a smaller portion of a large market, your persona might be 'young, active professionals, looking to create their own gardening business'.

Knowing your persona will impact on the type of content you write and the kind of tone of voice you use – and this is something we'll come to in a future chapter.

But at the same time, your persona is *also* going to define the kind of *place* that's ideal for you advertising.

In internet marketing there's a saying which is: be everywhere. Your ultimate objective is to have a very strong social media presence on every single big platform as well as to have your own website and really just finders in as many pies as humanly possible.

This is all good and well but unfortunately, it's also not terribly realistic for the small-time entrepreneurs. Eventually you might get there but in the short term, it makes a lot more sense to focus your efforts on one social network primarily and on one strategy primarily.

Again, this means thinking about the kind of person you're aiming at. The older generation for instance isn't all that likely to be on SnapChat or WhatsApp. Stats tell us that this is a younger person's game! If you want a hip young audience, then Instagram and SnapChat are the places to be. If you want earlier adopters/techies, then try out Periscope and live video streaming.

This will even affect the small details. If you're sending out emails as part of your email marketing campaign, then ask yourself what time of day your typical reader is likely to be most active!

CHAPTER 2

AUTHENTICITY WINS THE GAME

Now you've narrowed your focus and you know exactly who your audience is, you'll have a much more focussed strategy and this will give you a big advantage when it comes to standing out.

But with that said, you're still going to be up against a fairly tough challenge. Even in a less crowded niche there's still going to be thousands of people vying for the attention of your audience. Think about your own web experience: you can't go anywhere with ads flashing up, videos playing and billboards driving past you plastered to buses.

Everyone wants our attention and as a result, our brains have adapted. We're now desensitized to this kind of noise and thus far less likely to sit up and take any notice of *any* marketing campaign.

So how do you overcome this?

The answer is simple: be authentic, be different and offer value. Oh, and be interesting!

Don't be 'The Next Tim Ferriss'

The worst thing you can do if you want to stand out among all the noise is to try and set up another business model emulating one that already works.

The worst thing you can do is to become 'the next Tim Ferriss' or the 'the next Pat Flynn'.

When you do this, you quite simply aren't adding anything new to the mix. You're not differentiating yourself in any way and in fact you're going out of your way to be the same.

In a flock of sheep, which one stands out most? The black sheep of course! You need to be that black sheep and you need to swim against the tide.

That way, people will take notice of what you're doing because it will be interesting.

You won't just blend in among the background of noise.

This is another thing to consider when choosing your audience and your niche then: think about who you are, what you know and what you can bring to the table that no one else can.

Maybe you love fitness and comedy? Then how about a funny fitness channel?

Maybe your someone who is incredibly meticulous and you want to write about fashion. How about combining these things?

Don't be afraid to stand out and do something different, because it's what will make you interesting.

What You Can Learn from BuzzFeed

If you take a look at Facebook right now, then you'll find that there are a large number of posts from BuzzFeed being shared almost every single day on almost every single newsfeed. Likewise, there are many others that are quite similar to BuzzFeed in terms of the way they structure their titles and their links.

This is what is known in the industry as 'clickbait'.

Clickbait is anything that has been designed specifically to get clicked on and read and to get attention. And *normally* this type of content is very successful.

How does it work? Often by using titles that sound very exciting, that promise amazing things, that look controversial or that somehow spark curiosity. A good example of how you might spark curiosity is with this simple tweak to the normal 'list article' format:

Ten Unbelievable Ways to Lose Weight... Number 3 Changed My Life!

This works because it makes the reader stop and think about number three: what is it that changed this person's life? We also want to know what would make a weight loss method 'unbelievable'.

That then makes the person really want to click. This works much more that the very standard:

Ten Ways to Lose Weight Fast

Because quite frankly, we've seen that title hundreds of times and it just doesn't sound interesting or fresh any more.

Unfortunately, clickbait is very often just spam and when we *do* click on it, we often find that what's on the other side really doesn't deliver on what was promised.

As such, people are quickly becoming desensitized to this kind of content too.

And so that's *not* what I'm telling you to do.

Instead, what I'm telling you to do is to think about *why* this works and how you can adopt it.

And the answer is that two things make this approach work:

- It's different
- It's interesting

So make this your barometer when posting any kind of content: is it different and is it interesting? More importantly still, would you click on it if you saw it?

Then just make sure that your content really delivers on that promise: whether it's breaking news, a write up of a ground breaking scientific study, or some unique perspective on a subject that people find fascinating.

This is another example of why it pays to be different, unique and interesting and to be yourself. That way, your titles will *naturally* be clickbait without you having to get spammy about it!

CHAPTER 3

HOW TO USE STORIES TO WIN THE HEARTS OF YOUR AUDIENCE

There's another reason that the 'Number 3 Changed My Life' trick works so well though...

And that's because it's *personal*. It's a story. And we *love* being regaled by stories.

Look at these two titles and then decide which you'd rather read:

How to Make Thousands from a Mobile App How I Made $11,236 from a Mobile App

The first title is generic, it's removed and it's somewhat dull (let's be honest). The second title though? This one pops and it has immediate intrigue.

The main reason for this is that the second example tells a story. We know that we're going to learn not only how to make an app but also how it *feels* to have a successful app. That means we can imagine ourselves in that person's shoes and we can daydream about being successful app owners ourselves.

And as a story, it's likely to be much more engaging and interesting with a beginning, middle and end.

At the same time though, the latter option also has a number of other advantages. For starters, this option tells us that the person writing knows about apps and how to be successful *first hand*. This isn't an article written based on some general advice – this is an article that will recount exactly how someone *actually* managed to be that successful. We have a specific amount of money even which sounds very believable and real. It makes the source much more real and much more trustworthy.

More Benefits of Telling Stories

Telling stories works in a lot of other ways too.

What you have to recognize is that humans naturally relate to stories – it's a primitive thing and it's the way we've been passing on information for countless thousands of years. We used to sit around campfires regaling each other with tales of our adventures. But what we *didn't* do back then was tell people about how they too could 'earn $100 a day by clicking a few ads'. If you want to appeal to someone on a primal and basic level, then use the form of communication that has survived since the dawn of man!

Think about your own experience of stories and you'll know this to be true. Do you remember what it feels like to finish reading a book and to feel like you've been jolted out of a dream? Or to walk out of the cinema and have no idea what time of day it is? To be surprised to see it's gotten dark?

Stories can move us to tears, they can make us angry and they can make us laugh.

A cold sales pitch or 'Top 10 Ways to Lose Weight' just *can't* do this.

It's something that a surprisingly small number of bloggers and webmasters have caught onto but their loss is very much your gain!

This is just as important when it comes to selling as well. Start a sales pitch with:

"I was in the same position as you…"

And your readers will wake up, take notice and read on. This is FAR superior to starting the same sales letter with: "Introducing the best ebook on fitness"

Do you see the difference?

Building a Personal Brand

If you want to take this story idea and roll with it, then something you can do is to build a 'personal brand'. That means that the main brand for your website or for your business is going to be *you*. This in turn then frees you to write about your own experiences, to recount tales from your life and to speak directly to your audience.

In turn, everything you write will seem more relevant, more engaging and more fascinating and your audience will feel as though they know you – which definitely helps a great deal when it comes to winning their trust and making more sales/orders!

Personal brands also allow you to do a number of things on social media that you otherwise could not. For instance, you can now Tweet about your day, or upload pictures of Instagram of yourself in coffee shops/at the beach. You can let your fans get to know your dog, your friends, your partner – and all of this will help you to build a stronger connection with them. That's how you create *true* fans.

The Value Proposition

What all this *also* allows you to do is to focus on what's known as the 'value proposition'. Your value proposition is the thing that you are ultimately trying to sell and that means you're thinking about what your product, service or blog *does* for someone.

Let's put it another way: you don't sell hats, you sell warm heads.

And likewise, you don't sell fitness books: you sell abs. And you sell confidence.

And a great sex life.

You didn't buy this book because you wanted a file on your computer. You bought it because you wanted to be heard. You wanted your own platform. You wanted internet celebrity. Maybe you wanted financial independence.

It's the *feeling* that you're giving that really matters and very often this can relate to a lifestyle.

And this once again relates back to the target demographic and the persona. What lifestyle are you promoting? What lifestyle does your audience want? What are the things that they enjoy and respect?

If you have a fitness blog then you're selling the fitness lifestyle and that means healthy eating, energy, time outdoors, muscles and confidence.

If you have a gardening blog, then the lifestyle is probably more closely related to having a great home, to relaxing in the evening and to nurturing things to feel proud of. Maybe 'going green' is closely related and maybe you could even call this a 'natural lifestyle'.

Either way, once you identify the lifestyle you're promoting, you can then 'sell' that lifestyle through social media and through your personal brand.

Be consistent, but try to make your Facebook pages and your Instagram inspiring and encouraging for those people.

The photos you upload might be of you in the gym, or wearing clothes that look great *because* you go to the gym. Maybe you share photos of you playing with your dogs on the beach – because you're fit and healthy enough to do that. Maybe you share inspirational quotes on Twitter.

Likewise, for the gardening blog, you might want to share pictures of your plants. Maybe of healthy home-cooked dinners. Maybe of cosy nights in with the family. Or perhaps nice walks through areas of natural beauty.

In all these ways, you are selling your lifestyle and helping more people to buy into that promise. They will then want to get closer to you for the belief that in doing so, they can develop a similar lifestyle for themselves.

CHAPTER 4

BLOGGING - YOUR OWN PLATFORM
FOR BEING HEARD

Okay, now you know a lot of the strategy behind how you're going to get heard, it's time to actually start *executing* that plan.

And this starts with having your own platform and your own base of operations on the web. This will be the hub from which you promote all of your ideas and share all of those stories. And this will be the single easiest way for people to find you online.

So how do you build your blog? Let's go through some easy steps to make it easy...

Creating a Blog With WordPress

The simplest way to build a blog by far is by using WordPress. This is a 'CMS' (Content Management System) and a website builder. It's completely free and it's powerful enough that it's behind *most* of the biggest sites on the web. In fact, WordPress powers a whopping 25% of *all* websites and blogs on the net!

Best of all? It couldn't be easier to use and comes with endless support and expandability.

If you find an app on the web that's designed to help bloggers to reach bigger audiences or run their site more easily, then you can bet it's going to be aimed at *WordPress* users. Using anything else is just making life unnecessarily difficult – so make the wise choice.

Getting Set Up

Before you get set up, you'll first need your domain name and hosting account. You can get both these things through a hosting provider and what this will mean is that you have an address people can use to find you (your domain name) and a space to store your files online (your hosting). The easiest way to do this is to get both at the same time and this is what most hosting accounts will offer you when you go through the default options.

There are many different hosting companies out there, so you may want to spend some time comparing what you get and how much you pay. One thing you want to look for ideally though is something called 'CPanel'.

CPanel is a control panel that will come pre-installed on your server space and this will allow you to manage your site a lot more easily. One good example of a hosting account that comes with CPanel is Bluehost (www.bluehost.com).

BlueHost is a reliable choice for web hosting

When choosing your domain name, think very carefully. At this point, you need to select a brand for your website or business if you haven't already and this is something that's going to have a huge impact on your future fortunes.

A brand is not only a logo and a company name. More than that, it is a 'mission statement' and a set of values that ties all your products together. This is what will make people feel as though they know what to expect when they read one of your posts or buy one of your products and it is what will make your business into a movement that people can get behind, feel part of and feel excited about.

This ties in very closely with your value proposition and your target audience. How can you convey the lifestyle that you're selling immediately with a single word and a single image?

Spend some time working on this until you get something you're happy with and also make sure it's catchy, easily memorable and that it works well as the name of a website.

Installation

To install WordPress, all you now have to do is to log in to your CPanel and then look for the 'one click installs'. Here you'll see a one click installation option for WordPress and if you click that option, it will walk you through the steps necessary. Hit 'show advanced options' though and make sure you take the time to put in a password and username, as well as a name for the blog itself.

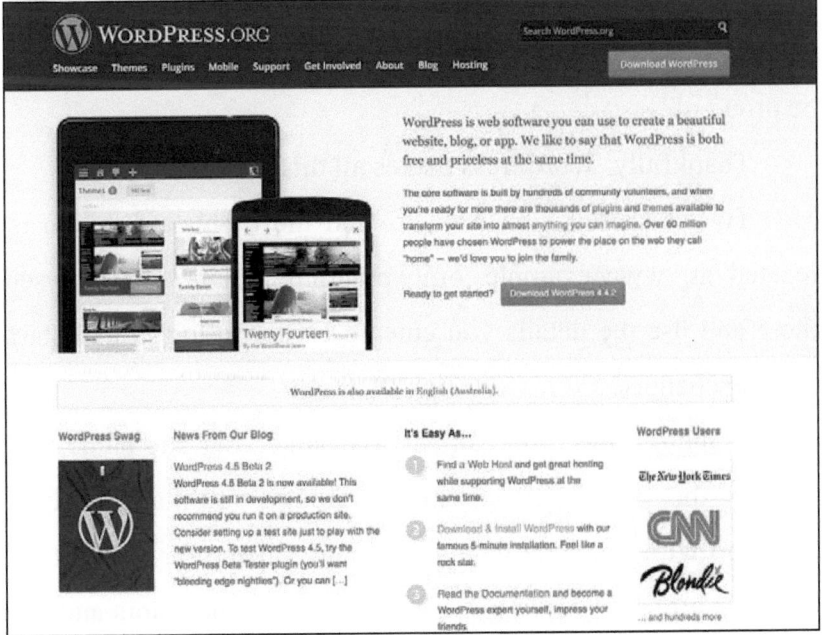

After a couple of seconds, your blog will now be installed and if you navigate to your domain, you'll see it there! It's a little empty at this point though...

Here's a step-by-step tutorial showing you how to start a blog using BlueHost:

http://unstoppableprofits.com/how-to-start-a-blog-in-5-minutes

Setting Up – And Basics of Good Design

Now you have a blog, it's time to start turning it into something people will actually want to look at and that you can be proud of.

Thankfully, WordPress makes all this pretty easy too!

To get started, you need to find the dashboard which is located at: www.example.com/wp-admin. Point your browser there and use the details you entered earlier to log in and start making changes.

In the settings, you can easily change your site name, the title and the 'blurb'. Along with this though, you'll also want to come up with a unique layout and colorscheme for your site – which is probably going to tie in closely with the colors and the look you selected for your log (if you have gotten to that point yet).

To manage this, you need to head over to 'Themes' and from there, you can browse through a wide array of different looks for your website. These will include free themes that you can install straight away as well as paid ones which will generally have a slightly more professional finish. Find something that works with your overall brand but remember that you will be able to customize this further later.

Another thing to make sure is that theme you pick is going to have a 'responsive design'. Responsive design means that a website changes shape and layout in order to conform to the size of the screen that it's being viewed on. Most themes will say if they are responsive (and most *should* be) and you can test this yourself by opening them in the browser (select 'Live Preview') and then changing the size of that window. It should move around to fit to the size dynamically and in that case, you know that it will look great on large monitors *and* tiny phone screens

Remember how we learned earlier that over 50% of web traffic came from mobile? That makes it *incredibly* important that you are catering to that audience.

There are a few more things to look for with your theme too. For starters, you should look for something with a nice large font that's crisp and easy to read on a high-contrast background. A sans-serif typeface that has a large font size and that's on a white background is a good starting point. This way, your site will be a pleasure to read. Your page should also load quickly and you should use large buttons instead of small hyperlinked text for your links – people need to be able to hit these buttons with their large fingers when they've just woken up!

Ultimately, when selecting your theme you need to ask yourself: can this complete with the very best content in your niche? Look at your top competitors and ask if your site is better than theirs. If it's not, then keep looking.

And if you want to find a wider selection of themes, note that you can also look on external sites. A good example is Theme Forest (www.themeforest.com).

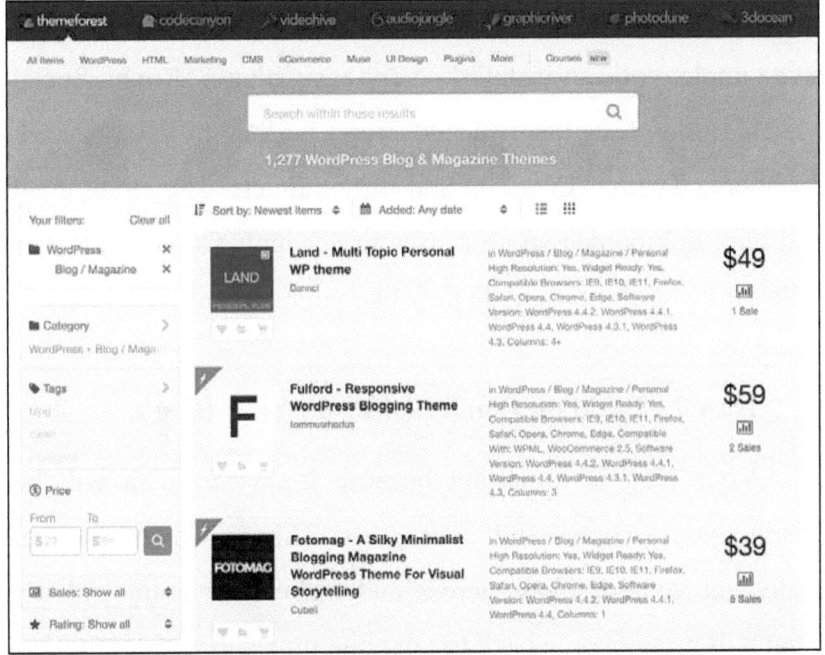

ThemeForest has a big range of Wordpress Themes to choose from

Plugins

Once you have your theme, you can also spend a little time looking through the plugins. These are small 'apps' that will run right on your site. They include widgets that appear in the sidebar and they include things that change your dashboard in order to give you more 'behind the scenes' options.

We'll talk about plugins a bit more later in this book but as an example, you can install the very basic plugin 'Round Social Media Buttons' which will add round buttons to your site for Facebook, Twitter, LinkedIn and Instagram etc. They look great and they link people straight to your accounts so they can start following you if they decide they like your content.

How To Build an Email List From Your Blog

Your blog is important because it's *where* you will be posting your articles and your posts. This is where you can really get your opinions across and make your point and it's what will bring people back to your site time and again.

At the same time though, this is also a good place for converting your one- off visitors into long-term fans. One of the best ways to do that is to collect emails, which you may recall as the number one marketing method in terms of ROI.

The aim here is simple: to get people to enjoy your content so much, that they decide they want more of it, that they don't want to miss future posts and that they want to be included in the VIP stuff that you put out.

So you need to keep delivering consistently high quality blog posts so that people will want to sign up. But you also need to make sure that they have the tools and the options in order to do that…

To get started then, you're going to need to get yourself an 'autoresponder'. An autoresponder is a piece of software that will manage your contacts and make it easier for you to send out emails to a large list. Not only does this let you send emails to hundreds or thousands of people at once without needing to use BCC – it also does things like allowing people to unsubscribe and filtering for spam. You can also use an autoresponder to send automated content from your blog, to monitor how many emails are being opened, to schedule messages and much more.

So you're going to need one and there are three main choices when it comes to choosing one: Aweber (www.aweber.com), MailChimp (www.mailchimp.com) and GetResponser (www.getresponse.com). There are other options, some of which are cheaper (or even free), but these three major players have the most support from plugins and external features so it's worth signing up for one of these accounts

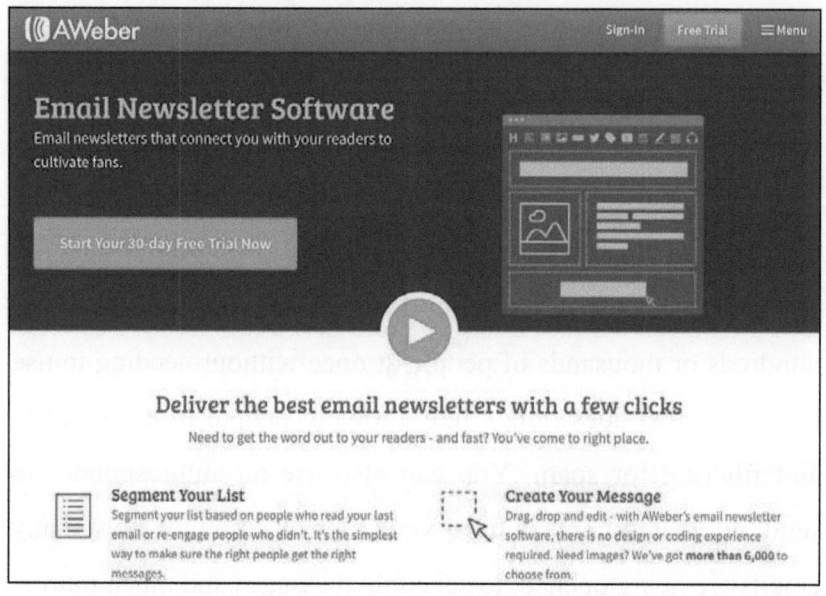

Now you'll be able to make your 'opt-in' form, which is the form your users can use to sign up. Make sure this is placed prominently on your site: add it to the bottom of your blog posts, put it in your sidebar as a widget and even use a plugin like SumoMe in order to have it show up in a pop-over window when people visit your page.

Another trick? *Talk* about your mailing list regularly in your blog posts and even on your social media. Tell people how you have exciting content on the way 'if you're a subscriber' and tell people why they should bother to sign up. Don't just leave your opt-in form quietly and expect people to sign up of their own accord – give them reasons to and make sure they *can't* miss that form!

Creating an Incentive

One more great strategy is to add an incentive to your mailing list. This can be something like a 'free report' and the idea is that your audience will get access to the free content and the free information in exchange for handing over their details and letting you message them further in future. Using an incentive is a great way to convince people to sign up if they were previously on the fence about it and it can help you to make a lot more money.

But at the same time, you also need to make sure people aren't *only* signing up for the incentive. Really the 'best' incentive is that they want to hear from you more and they're excited to receive your correspondence. Make your incentive a nice added bonus and not the main attraction – it will result in a more targeted list!

CHAPTER 5

HOW TO CREATE A SOCIAL MEDIA PLAN

Now your blog is in place and you're starting to collect lots of emails, all you need to do is to send more people there.

And one of the best ways you can possibly do this is with a social media strategy. At the same time, having a plan on social media will also allow you to stay visible to your audience even when you're not posting. If someone is following you on Facebook and Twitter, then you can greatly increase your brand recognition and make sure you're at the forefront of your customers' minds at all times. This then in turn means that when they decide they need a product or service that you provide – you will be the first person they come to in order to get it!

So the question is: how do you go about creating that plan and conquering social media?

Regularity, Quality, Consistency

Perhaps the easiest way to think about this is to start by looking at what *doesn't* work. And for that we have any number of examples from companies all over Facebook, Twitter and Instagram.

The problem for these companies is that they often focus on just one thing: promoting their products and services. They create their social media account, they do a *little* promotion to encourage people to follow them and then they just occasionally post messages like:

"Our drain cleaning products are second to none!" "That's why Mums love NappyMate!"

It's just bad marketing and again the reason is that it fails to pass the ultimate litmus test: you wouldn't follow it yourself.

Think about the brands and the pages you *are* following on Facebook and most likely you'll find that they're brands and pages that regularly post content that you find interesting. If you're into fitness then you'll enjoy getting articles about staying healthy sent to your wall and if you're into poetry then maybe you follow a Twitter account that posts short poetry.

In other words, there's something in it for you and you're receiving *value*.

That value can come in the form of entertainment, it can come in the form of information or it can come in the form of discounts. Either way though, you're getting something consistent and in that way you can feel almost as though the social account is providing you with a service.

If a social media page is done well, then people should be upset when it goes for a long time without any new updates. If people are happy when they don't see another post from you in a while then you know you're doing something wrong!

Why it's Important To Be Consistent

Let's imagine an example revolving around a life insurance company. Now if the life insurance company were to use the same marketing strategy as 99% of the other insurance companies, then it would probably just post regularly about how people need to look after their family and how they have the best rates.

That's not great and no one is going to want to follow that!

So instead, a smart life insurance company might identify its small corner of the market. In this case, we're going to say that it's targeting single Mums.

Mums are generally women and seeing as Pinterest is a social media platform that appeals to women more than men, this might be a good place to focus on that wouldn't be too crowded.

Now, instead of just trying to drown Pinterest in sales pitches, the company *instead* makes the decision to provide a real, useful service on that platform. It creates a blog that talks about the challenges of being a single Mum and it *also* uses Pinterest as a place to post images that suggest activities for small families. The photos are at once inspiring, promoting a happy-family lifestyle but at the same time, they're helpful in that they offer useful advice.

If people see these pictures and like them, they'll follow the account. And because the account is delivering consistent quality, they'll stay following, share that content and look out for future posts.

And thus, when the account talks about how its followers can exclusively get 20% off their life insurance – it will get a massive response.

Do you see the difference? You have the ear of a massive audience because you're offering something useful, inspiring and interesting that's perfectly catered to your audience.

In order to make the sales and get the attention, you have to offer something worthwhile in return.

How to Post Regularly

And in order for this method to work, you also of course need to post regularly and consistently.

Because if you only post once every few weeks, you'll struggle to get the momentum going. And when someone looks at your social media page, they'll question whether you're even still going!

At the same time, your posts need to be consistently on the same topic. If every third picture on that life insurance page was of Optimus Prime, then it would be confusing for the audience and a lot of people would leave.

So know what you do, do it well and do it consistently.

There's just one problem though, right? You're probably worrying at this stage about how long this is all going to take. That's a fair point, but fortunately there are a large number of tools available that can help us to save a lot of time posting to social media and help us to ensure that we never miss a beat.

Let's look at a few of them here:

Mobile

Most social media sites have mobile apps that you can use instead and this is especially useful if you are building a personal brand. Using the camera on your phone you can simply snap pictures for Instagram, while Tweeting about your day takes all of two minutes. This helps keep your feed alive and again keeps you at the forefront of your followers' minds.

Scheduling

There are a few different tools you can use in order to schedule your posts. One example is Hootsuite (www.hootsuite.com) and another is Buffer (www.buffer.com). In some cases, such as with Facebook, the social media site itself will come with scheduling as a built-in option.

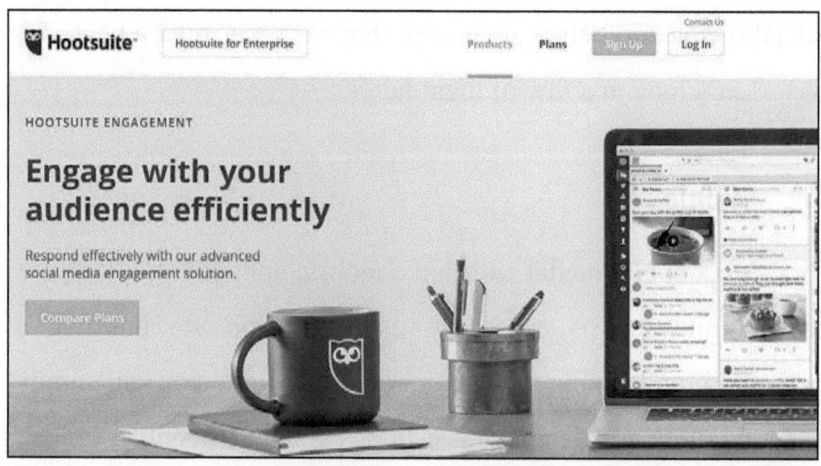

What this basically means, is that you can sit down when you have some free time one afternoon and then you can write out hundreds of posts for your page. You then enter these into the tool of your choice and it will drip- feed them out to your followers.

You can still manually publish new content if you want to as well but this way you now know for certain that you'll never go a month without thinking of anything witty to say. Likewise, you'll save a lot of time by writing all this fresh content in one sitting and not having to keep uploading it and starting afresh.

IFTTT

IFTTT (www.ifttt.com) stands for 'If This, Then That' and is an incredibly powerful tool. We won't go into it in massive depth right now but suffice to say that you can link all your different social media accounts and web apps. It's actually incredible how many interactions you can set up this way. On a very basic level for instance, you can make your Twitter posts post to Facebook as well, or you can save your Instagram pictures in Dropbox. But if you wanted to get advanced and strange, you could set up a Philips Hue lighting system and then create an interaction so that every time someone liked your page, your lighting changed color. This could be used for all kinds of fun marketing and it has a lot of practical purposes too. If you're going to look into this, then get the mobile app too and Tasker for Android to really increase the power and the options.

Planning Tools

While automation is handy up to a point, you still need to simply find the time to work – though thankfully there are tools out there to help with this too. For instance you can schedule yourself some time to work in Google Calendar, or why not use something tailor made for this kind of job such as coschedule (www.coschedule.com) or Asana (www.asana.com).

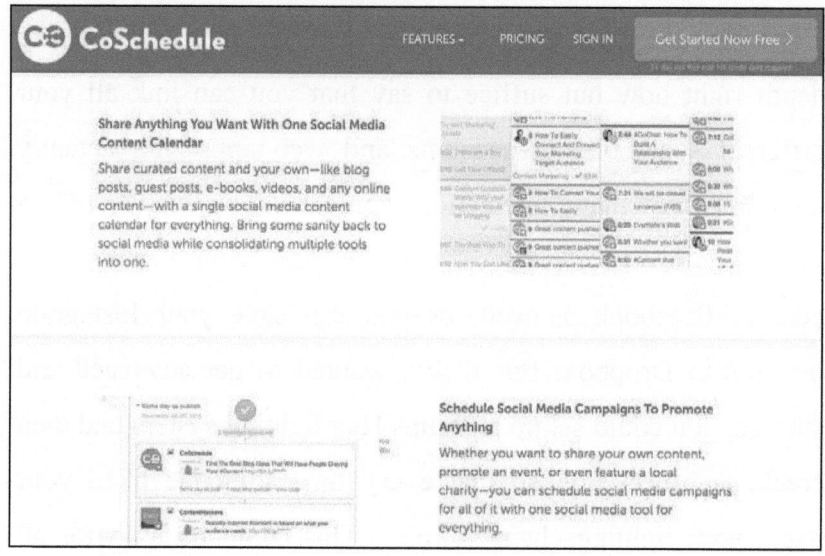

Statistics and Analysis

What's most important of all is that you're looking at the reports for all your social media efforts and that you know precisely what's working and what isn't. Most social media sites like Facebook have these features built in (in Facebook, go to your page and then select 'Page Insights' along the top). You can also use third party software for more in-depth analysis such as 'LikeAlyzer' (www.LikeAlyzer.com). All this will allow you to see which of your posts performs best, which of your followers are most engaged and how quickly you're gaining new fans. At the end of the day, the objective is to do more of what's working and less of what's not!

It's also worth researching general statistics to find out things like when's the best time to post. You can find a great guide to that topic for Facebook here:

https://www.quicksprout.com/2016/02/05/how-to-win-on-facebook-8- lessons-learned-from-analyzing-1-billion-posts/.

Strangely, it seems the best times to post are at 9 pm-11 pm in the evening and there's another nice spike between 9 am-10 am.

But while this kind of resource is very useful, you should also bear in mind a couple of things. First: when you post isn't necessarily when you get seen. Second: different audiences behave differently (we touched on this earlier). Third: you need to think about time zones. That's why using the above tools is the best way to know for certain what's working for you and what you need to focus on.

CHAPTER 6

THE TYPES OF CONTENT TO SHARE
ON SOCIAL MEDIA THAT YOUR AUDIENCE
WILL THANK YOU FOR

We've already discussed the types of posts that work really well on social media in terms of blogs that will get you clicks (just to recap: you want to write posts that are unique, different, interesting and that have an emotional reaction).

But what about the rest? Unless you are a prolific writer you're not going to be able to create multiple new blog posts every single day and that's going to limit the amount of exposure you get.

Posting regularly to Facebook in particular is actually very important too, seeing as only somewhere between 5-15% of your audience will see your content each time you post.

So you need to post a lot. What do you say?

Deals and Offers

While you mustn't just promote yourself as we've covered at length, surveys show that audiences *do* respond very well to special deals and special offers. The caveat is that the offers should actually be impressive and that they should be exclusive to your audience. This way, you are rewarding them for their loyalty by offering something that no one else is getting.

This is also a great way to buy yourself some good will too – so think hard about ways that you can impress your audience with your offers. Don't just offer money off: how about doing something different such as personalizing your product or service? Or offering some kind of limited edition product?

O2 is a phone company in the UK that partners with other businesses in order to offer its customers all *kinds* of special deals and offers. Better yet, it combines this with an app that has access to GPS so that a user can be walking down the street when they get offered a free chocolate from the store they're passing, or a £1 lunch (about $2).

This kind of marketing works well because those customers now have a very real incentive to keep listening to the messages they get from that company and because they'll feel genuinely rewarded and VIP each time they capitalize on one of those special offers or deals. It can actually make your day to be given a free rose on Valentine's Day!

Think about how you can spoil your followers rotten!

Links to Other Posts

Running out of posts that you can upload? Then how about uploading posts from other creators? There's nothing wrong with just sharing posts that other people have written and from other websites – it won't gain you traffic but it *will* help you to continue offering that great service to your audience.

Better yet, is that there are tools out there that can help you to find the most trending topics in your niche. A good example is 'BuzzSumo' while you can also find trending posts on Facebook by looking at the top right of your newsfeed. As these posts are trending and have lots of shares, you know for a fact that they're popular and you know for a fact that they thrive well on social media. That in turn means that you can now upload them and expect to get lots of Likes and Shares as well – leading to lots more exposure for your brand.

Videos and Images

Remember earlier how we said that you could use photos from your daily life in order to promote a lifestyle and to create a personal brand that would let people feel as though they know you personally?

This is a great strategy but there are other ways you can do similar things too. For example, why not use SnapChat in order to update your followers with short videos of you talking to the camera and sharing your opinion?

You can do the same thing through Vine and both types of media can easily then be posted to Facebook or Instagram.

What this does is it allows you to speak directly with your audience but it only takes you a couple of seconds to make something new!

Downloads and Freebies

Don't just use PDFs and other giveaways as bribes! Why not give something away for real without asking anything in return? Again this builds great good will and it establishes you as a page worth watching.

Legacy Content

You don't only have to post about your latest new article. If you have an article that was successful a year ago then why not remind people of it by posting it again? There's no reason it can't have a second lease of life.

Updates

You can also update people about your lifestyle and give them a bit of an insight into who you are just by posting about your day, the challenges you're facing or perhaps witty asides that you've thought of. Again, this is showing the real you and your human side and is helping people to feel as though they know you. While this all works though, make sure that you are still remaining on topic (largely) and that you're reinforcing the lifestyle that you're trying to promote.

In other words, if your website is all about natural living, don't post about how you just enjoyed eating a massive McDonald's and likewise don't post about the latest Avenger's movie. Stay on topic and avoid verbal diarrhoea!

Memes and Inspirational Photos

These can be built easily and they happen to share *very* well.

Engaging With Your Audience

Another important aspect of posting to social media is to make sure that you're engaging with your audience and actually talking to them.

The mistake is to think of social media as a podium for you to shout from. This isn't something you should be using for one-way communication but rather should be thought of as a tool for facilitating *conversation*. After all, social media is a communication tool first and foremost and should be used as such.

So there's nothing wrong with asking your audience what *they* think about a topic. Post an interesting article and then ask for feedback. Or poll your audience on a controversial or divisive question.

You can also use social media in order to run contests and promotions. For instance, create a contest where you award a big discount to one of your followers once you reach '1,000 likes'. This can be a great way to get more attention and buzz surrounding your brand and also to get people to do some free promotion for you!

Instagram is a particularly great place for running promotions. For example, you can invite your followers to upload pictures of themselves using your brand or living the lifestyle you promote and then award one of them with a price and some free exposure. In doing this, you will once again expose all of the followers of all of the participants to what you're all about – while the followers themselves will feel more involved and more excited for your brand than ever before!

You can even use your social media page in order to do market research and to get advice that you'll use to help steer the direction of your business. Not sure what your next product should be? Then just ask your audience what they want to see! If you create a product that your audience has literally asked you to make, then there's very little chance of it not selling!

This is called 'crowdsourcing' and it's one of the 'big ideas' that businesses are getting excited about right now.

CHAPTER 7

HOW TO CREATE CONTENT THAT GETS SHARES

Wait a second, didn't we also talk about this?

No: we talked about how to create content that gets *clicked*. And content that gets clicked works differently from content that gets shared.

But having your content shared *should* be one of the ultimate aims for your brand online. The reason for this is that getting shared can lead to exponential growth in your user-base and potentially even help something you create to 'go viral'. (Going viral is defined as being shared a million times, which of course is rather beneficial for *any* business!)

This is taking full advantage of the very nature of social media. The great thing about social media is that it mimics real life social networks and the way that memes and ideas spread through them. If you create a post and upload it to Facebook, the hope is that 10 of your followers might Like it, share it or comment on it.

When this happens, that post then becomes visible to all the people that are connected to *those* users. So now your exposure has just grown by 1,000%! And if 10 of the friends of each of those ten people shares your content, then you'll be seen by 10,000% more… and it keeps growing!

So how do you go about creating content that will go viral and get shared that much? Or how do you at least make something that will get shared a little bit…

The Psychology of Sharing

It all comes down to psychology and to understanding *why* people share in the first place.

And to understand this, we need to revisit a concept from right at the start of this book: the persona.

As you'll hopefully recall, a persona is a fictional biography that describes the individual that your post, your product or your service is for.

When you're creating content that you want to share well on social media, you need to keep this persona in mind at all times. It can help to imagine someone you know in the real world who is just like that person. Keep them in your mind as you write and imagine that you are sat opposite them and explaining the subject directly to them.

This will lead to a more engaging post and it will lead to something that is highly targeted at your specific end user.

But that's not where the magic lies.

The magic lies in what happens when you share this content and someone reads it.

And again we need to go back to something we said earlier: Social media is primarily a tool for communication.

The reason this is relevant is simple: people *share* because they're communicating. When someone shares your post, they are doing it *as* a form of communication.

This means that they either share the content with their audience, or a specific friend because they think they're going to enjoy it; OR they share it on their own wall as a form of self-expression. In both scenarios, other people and communication are at the heart of their motivation.

And this is why having a previse persona in mind is so useful and important.

Let's imagine your persona is 'anyone who works from home'. So you've written a blog post that is perfectly targeted at people who work from home and that addresses things they might go through. Let's say you've called it:

'This is Why Your Friends Struggle to Work From Home'

Or perhaps:

'Five Life-Changing Tips for People Who Work From Home'

Now you've created that title, it's perfectly clear *who* that post is aimed at. Now, when you share it to your followers, some of those people reading are going to identify strongly with the title. They identify as someone who works from home and they probably enjoy that fact about themselves. Thus, by sharing that content with their friends, they are communicating that they relate to your post and telling their audience something about them.

But there's another kind of person who will share this content too: the kind of person who *knows* someone who works from home. Because the article is so clearly targeted at a particular persona and because the second one offers to provide value, you might think: 'this will be useful for Jeff'. Thus, you share it to Jeff's wall and you thereby help out Jeff and show you're thinking of him – making your friendship stronger.

Either way, your post has facilitated that.

Personas, Titles and Routes to Market

Notice how we're bringing this all together nicely here? It really is simple once you land on that formula and it helps in a ton of ways.

Because when you're writing for a persona, you'll also be creating more routes to market for your posts. One great example? Social communities.

For example, if you write an article called 'What Writers Can Learn From Bruce Lee', then you've created something with two very interesting personas: writers and martial artists.

This then means that you can share your post in a number of interesting places in order to reach a huge audience that will be perfectly targeted for that post. Join a Google+ community or a Facebook Page that's all about Bruce Lee for instance and post there and you'll probably get a hundred Likes or more.

Another great option is Reddit which is all about finding specific audiences with particular interests.

This is a great way to find smaller sections of your audience and to hone in on them too. Maybe you *did* pick a large niche for your blog like 'Making Money Online' – but that doesn't mean that you can't target your *articles* at smaller sections of your market like work-from-home Mums or students who want to start online businesses. Write articles specifically for them and share them to these online communities that will provide your routes to market.

More Ways to Get Likes and Shares

Of course that's not all there is to getting likes and shares – there are a number of other hints and tricks too.

For example, remember how we said you could use BuzzSumo in order to share *other people's* content? Well how about using that same tool as a way to come up with ideas for your own content? Don't copy anything you see is doing well here but rather look at it and see which niches and which titles are doing particularly well. Now you can write something in a similar tone or on a similar concept and hopefully enjoy the same success.

Looking at what's trending is also a very good idea and especially on Twitter and Instagram where a topical hashtag can make *all* the difference.

You can also empower others to share your content. For instance, try using the plugin in Shareaholic (www.shareaholic.com). This will add social sharing buttons to your blog posts on WordPress, meaning that people who enjoy your content can share it quickly with others on Facebook or on Twitter.

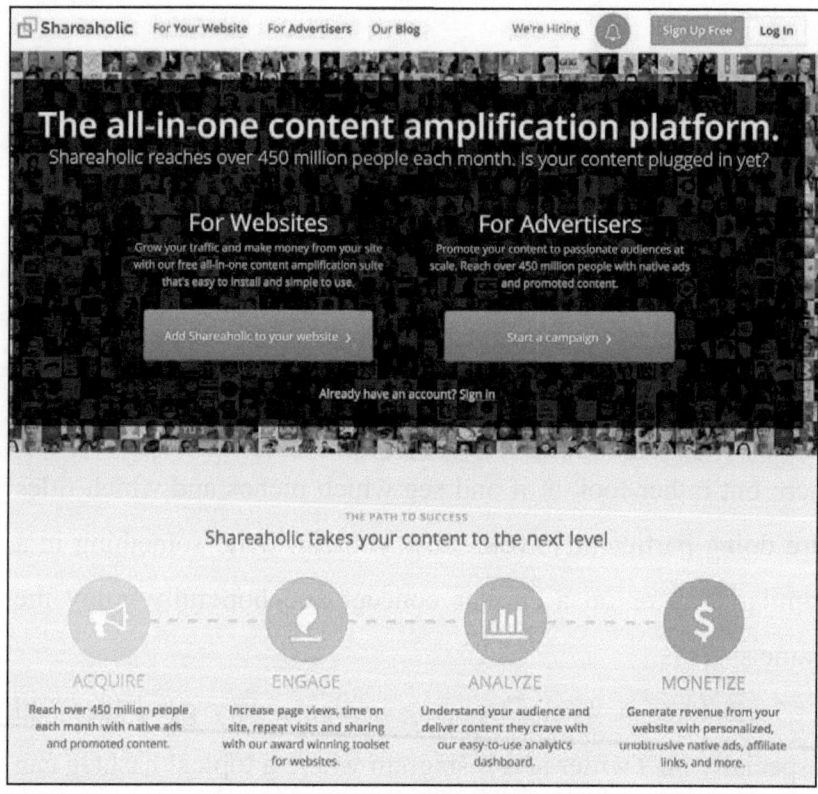

And don't forget to simply *ask* people to share your content too! This is something that people do an awful lot on

YouTube and it can work well on your blog too. Write the best blog post you can possibly write and then at the end just say:

"If you loved this blog post then please consider Liking it on Facebook. It helps me a great deal and that way, I'll be able to keep updating you with more awesome posts!"

Sometimes you just gotta' ask!

CHAPTER 8

10 TACTICS FOR GETTING MORE FOLLOWERS

This is a great set of steps that you can rinse and repeat over and over to keep getting more followers. Write new posts with a persona in mind, share them on social media, promote them in relevant groups – ask for help!

That will help you to keep gathering momentum and building a bigger and bigger audience – but sometimes you'll also want a 'shot in the arm' to help you along your way. Here are ten tactics to help you build even more followers:

1. Influencer Marketing

Influencer marketing is massive right now in the world of internet marketing and that's for one very good reason: it works!

Influencer marketing simply means that you are going to find someone who is already very big and very influential in your niche and then you're going to get them to give you a shout-out. This then means you gain immediate exposure to their entire audience, rather than having to spend all that time building up to it.

The only problem? Getting an influencer to respond to you can be tricky. Don't go straight for the top dog then but rather build yourself up gradually by going from one tier to the next!

2. Become Active on a Forum

If you can become very active and well-respected on a forum, then you'll be able to give yourself a huge head start when you launch your blog and/or business. This is because you'll have people who consider you almost a *friend* and they'll not only want to read what you put out but may also help you to promote your work! Read '1,000 True Fans' and you'll see how life changing this can be for a small business.

3. Find an Angle, Write Press Releases

Another trick is to come up with an interesting story or feature about your blog. Maybe it's the story of how you got started or maybe you're going to blog about something that's really unique. If it's interesting enough, then it might be worth writing some press releases and sending them to big websites and magazines in your niche.

4. Guest Post

A guest post is a post that you write on another blog in exchange for a link back. It's sort of an example of influencer marketing but it's a lot easier to find people who will play ball!

5. Pay for Advertising

If you have the budget, then paying for advertising is of course a viable option. This is especially true if you pay for Facebook ads which utilize all the benefits we've already learned about Facebook. Not only can your ads potentially spread virally but they can be perfectly targeted toward a specific audience based on age, sex, location and other demographics!

6. Create Quizzes

One type of content that does very well on social media is the quiz. Remember: people love expressing themselves and talking about who they are and a quiz lets them do that perfectly – especially if they can share the answers.

7. Add Your Feeds to Your Blog

You can use plugins and widgets for WordPress in order to have not only your social media *links* on your blog but also feeds from those profiles. For instance, you can show off your most recent Instagram pictures in the sidebar or have all your Twitter posts appear there! Not only does this show your viewers your social media channels and entice them to follow you but it also ensures that your WordPress site stays looking active and interesting.

8. Use Linkbait

You know what clickbait is, now can you guess what linkbait is? This is anything that entices other blogs and forum members to link to your site.

What kind of content works as linkbait? One good example is anything controversial – which is often useful for sparking debates. Another good option is something that provides a definite guide with lots of resources. This way, if someone wants to learn something, forum members can simply point them to the resource you've created. Note that the ideal length for a blog post in the eyes of Google is 1,800 words – that's pretty in-depth!

9. Choose Your Images Wisely

Something that may surprise you is that a lot of people share content on social media before they've even read it! And the same goes for hitting that Like button. People assume it's going to say X and they share on that basis.

This means that first impressions are *everything* for your post. One way to use this to your advantage is to use a great image. Ideally you want an image so good that people will Like the image alone, regardless of the content!

10. Use Facebook Comments

Another very cool plugin you can use is Facebook Comments. This adds a comments section to your blog posts which lets people discuss what you've written right there on the page. This is a great way to build an active community on your page and to keep people coming back.

What's even better though, is that this is *Facebook* comments. That means that people can login using their Facebook details and don't have to sign up. And it also means that people can choose to share the comments they post to their Facebook page for their friends etc. to see.

Note of course that it's also very useful to learn other forms of marketing. And particularly useful in this regard are things like SEO – Search Engine Optimization – which will help you to get more visitors from Google. This is a whole book in itself but suffice to say that adding lots of great content is a very good start!

CONCLUSION and SUMMARY

And there you have it, the ultimate guide to *being heard*. If you've felt that using the web is a little like speaking to a brick wall, then this will help you to start getting noticed and actually getting some pay off for all your hard work.

Here's a short recap of what we looked at:

• Finding your audience and choosing a demographic that you can market to

• Looking for routes to market and using your existing contacts

• Identifying a persona

• Thinking about the competition

• Creating a blog

• Building a brand

• Designing your blog to reflect that brand

• Finding the right social media outlet for you

• Delivering a 'service' through your social media

- Being consistent
- Using tools and plugins to help you be consistent
- Growing your channel

Now if you want to start putting that advice into practice, here are some steps to get you started:

1. Choose your niche, your brand, your mission statement and your audience. Think about a smaller amount of competition but also about what makes *you* unique and what *you're* interested in.

2. Get a domain and hosting and build a WordPress site.

3. Design that site and add a mailing list.

4. Set up social media profiles and choose a few to focus on based on your target demographic.

5. Consider how you're going to offer value to that audience.

6. Post regularly and consistently while providing value.

7. Think about targeting specific users with specific posts.

8. Look for online communities and places to share your content.

9. Add social sharing tools to your site.

10. Consider using advanced growth strategies like influencer marketing.

Do all that and your site will have the very best shot of growing and helping you to be heard. Of course global stardom doesn't come overnight though, so keep at it and stay vigilant.

If you love what you do and if you're truly passionate about your topic, then you'll eventually be successful!

You have your megahorn – now you just need to decide what you want to say!

IMPORTANT: To help you further take action, print out a copy of the *Checklist* and *Mindmap* I provided. You'll also find a Resource Cheat Sheet with valuable sites, posts and articles that I recommend you go through.

9 786069 836873

Printed by Libri Plureos GmbH in Hamburg,
Germany